BALLET STEPS

BALLET STEPS
PRACTICE TO PERFORMANCE

Antony Dufort

Clarkson N. Potter, Inc./Publishers NEW YORK

DISTRIBUTED BY CROWN PUBLISHERS, INC.

Acknowledgments

Of the many people who helped me in different ways, I would especially like to thank the following:

Peter Wright, Sadler's Wells Royal Ballet. Peter Schaufuss, London Festival Ballet. Harold King and Heather Knight, London City Ballet, who kindly allowed me to attend company classes and Kate Castle, Dance Education Officer at The Royal Ballet. Susan Cooper of the Royal Academy of Dancing and Deborah Bull who patiently answered all my questions but must not be held responsible for any errors! Without them I would not have got very far. Vincent Hantam, Jonathan Cope, Viviana Durante, Errol Pickford, Wayne, Nicky, Anita, Jacquie, Debbie and Karen, all modelled for the illustrations. Luke Jennings was the greatest help at an early stage in the project. Nic Barlow, Alex Dufort, Hugh Palmer, Jamie Muir and Richard Sparks gave me invaluable advice concerning photography and video. Bill Cooper and Leslie Spatt were enormously helpful with finding suitable performance photographs to go with my drawings. finally, I would like to thank Jesse Graham, Kate Gardiner, Clare Park, Sharon McGorian, Elisabetta Brodasca, and Caradoc King.

Originally published in Great Britain by Phoebe Phillips Editions, 6 Berners Mews, London W1P 3DG, England.

Published in the United States in 1985 by Clarkson N. Potter, Inc., One Park Avenue, New York, 10016 and simultaneously in Canada by General Publishing Company Limited.

Clarkson N. Potter, Potter, and colophon are trademarks of Clarkson N. Potter, Inc.

A PHOEBE PHILLIPS EDITIONS BOOK
Printed and bound in Great Britain

Library of Congress Cataloging-in-Publication Data

Dufort, Antony.
Ballet steps.

Includes index.
1. Ballet dancing. I. Title.
GV1788.D84   1985   792.8'2   85-9559
ISBN 0-517-55522-0

10 9 8 7 6 5 4 3 2 1

First American Edition

Dedication

In memory of my father Timothy Dufort and my grandmother Doris Travis (née de Halpert),
a wonderful painter who taught me everything I know,
and also Louise Abbott and Adam Sedgewick.

 L Ballo è un'arte di muovere
ordinatamente il corpo, af-
fine di piacere agli fpetta-
tori.

'Ballet is the Art of moving the body according to certain
laws of harmony, in a way pleasing to the audience.'
GIAMBATTISTA DUFORT   Trattato del Ballo Nobile   Napoli 1728

Preface

For most people who develop a passionate interest in the ballet, being taken at the age of five ore six to see THE NUTCRACKER or THE SLEEPING BEAUTY at Christmas seems to have been a turning point in their lives. I was not so lucky.

I didn't see my first ballet until I was twenty-seven. Stuck up in the 'gods' at The Royal Opera House in Covent Garden with half the stage and most of the scenery hidden from view, I couldn't see very much, and understanding almost nothing about the dancer's art, I was not inspired by the little I did see. Some years later I had another look at the programme from that night and discovered that I had been watching Anthony Dowell and Antoinette Sibley at the height of their powers, in Sir Kenneth MacMillan's production of ROMEO AND JULIET.

Happily, in spite of my lack of appreciation a persistent friend took me to watch a company class, followed by a rehearsal. This was a revelation. Here were people I understood, real people, working with extreme dedication at the elements of their art.

In fact, I had already used dancers as models for drawings and sculpture, because they are so much more aware of how their bodies look from any angle. They are particularly good too, at holding a pose. But now, for the first time, I was looking at the fascinating variety of their shapes and movements as they exercised and rehearsed in class, and I wanted to draw and sculpt them at their work.

I found it almost impossible at first because the movements seemed to go by so quickly. I began to search for a book which would explain something of the formal language of classical ballet in a way that I would be able to understand: a book that would also explain the connections between what I saw in the classroom and the performances that I now began to watch with increasing interest on the stage.

There are many beautiful ballet books. Unfortunately they are either large and glossy, based mainly on dramatic photographs, or small and technical, full of stick-figures and outline sketches that only a professsional dancer would understand. None of them seemed to capture that flow of movement which is so important in the art of dance.

Because the book I was looking for did not exist, I was forced to undertake my own research, and BALLET STEPS began.

Classical ballet is an expressive language which uses music, the human body, and the inspiration of the dancer and choreographer. Writing and illustrating BALLET STEPS has helped me to understand something of this language. I hope it will also help young dancers and their parents, and ballet-goers of all ages, to gain an understanding of the basic elements of dance and its special vocabulary. Above all, I hope it will increase enjoyment of one of the great arts of our day.

Antony Dufort

Contents

Introduction

For most of us, the image of a girl standing on *pointe* sums up perfectly what makes classical ballet so different from any other form of dance. Her shape has a mysterious quality; a flowing elegant line runs upwards from her toe, through her body, into her upraised arm and beyond. There is a feeling of balance and harmony, of effortless co-ordination. To the spectator it seems so easy, so natural, that he hardly pauses to wonder how it is done. And this is how it should be: for classical ballet is one art form for which outstanding technique is a minimum requirement. In fact, holding a position like this needs tremendous effort; and it is a tribute to the dedication and training of every professional dancer that this is the last thing we think of when watching a ballet.

It seemed natural to base BALLET STEPS on the daily class and rehearsals which make up so much of the dancer's working life, and the special training which makes ballet possible.

For me the class is fascinating. Watching dancers exercise in ordinary leotards, uncluttered by costume, makes everything clearer. So this is how I have drawn them. Slow movements, fast jumps and turns – all are broken down into a series of drawings across the page; and this conveys far more movement than a single dramatic photograph. The small stage-photographs complete the picture, connecting practice with performance.

I took photographs first, and based my drawings on them. This way I was free to correct those tiny mistakes that spoil the classical line – a hand or a foot, even just a finger slightly out of place.

Choosing what steps to illustrate and which to leave out was very difficult. Even with a book ten times as thick as this and years more to do the drawings, I would still not have covered the full range of ballet steps. So, with the help of dancer friends and consultants, I have had to be very selective.

I had three principal aims: first of all, the steps had to be common enough for the spectator to spot in most popular classical ballets. Second, I wanted to show representative examples of all the different types of movement that the dancer is expected to master, as a soloist or in the *corps de ballet*. Third, I wanted to show what makes the *pas de deux* so exhilarating – the flow of movement and the greater range of shapes that two bodies can make when moving in harmony or counterpoint. As the world knows, certain partnerships have brought an extra magic to the dance which has delighted a whole generation of spectators not previously interested in the ballet.

Through their own original and creative interpretations of the great roles, dancers keep classical ballet alive and fresh and exciting. For all their rigorous training, their continual striving for perfection, ballet dancers are not robots. Sometimes, in the brilliance of a major production, dancers appear almost superhuman to us. They are not, of course. They are human beings as well as artists – but human beings who work, perhaps, a little harder than the rest of us . . .

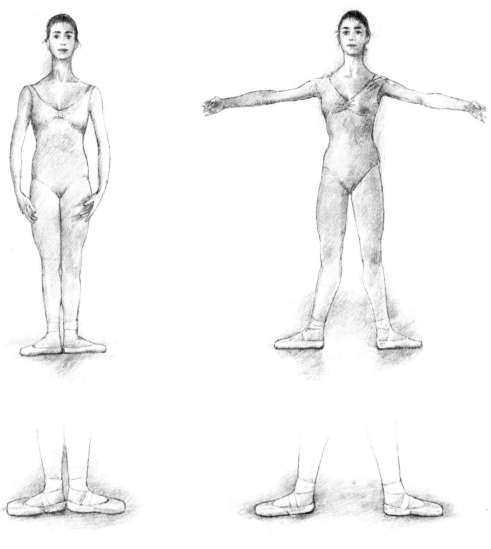

First position

Second position

The Basic Positions   Young dancers are taught the five positions of the arms and feet during their earliest lessons. They form the basis of all classical choreography, and therefore of classical training. Each position has its own particular qualities, and most steps start, finish and pass through one or more of them.

Different movements of the legs, to the front, the back and the sides are possible with each of the five positions, but there are certain qualities that they all share.

The body is perfectly poised; its weight is evenly distributed over both feet; the muscles of the legs are 'pulled up' and the legs and feet are

14

Third position   Fourth position   Fifth position

fully *turned out* to the side. At the same time, the upper body is relaxed and free, allowing the arms to move gracefully without any hint of strain. It is difficult for very young dancers to do the *fourth* and *fifth positions* at first, so they may do the *third position* instead. Professional dancers do not need to use the *third position* very often.

The *turn out* of the legs is such a vital part of classical ballet technique, that it needs to be understood in more detail.

Turn Out   At first glance, *turned out* feet
look just like Charlie Chaplin's, and you may
think that this is just what the dancer on the left
looks like as he goes down into a *plié* with his
feet turned completely out to the side. In fact he,
and the dancer on the right, have rotated not just
their feet but the whole of their legs, from the
hip right through to the toe. This is what dancers
call *turn out*.

There are a lot of movements in ballet where
the legs have to be lifted very high in the air in
different directions. Without ballet training this
would be very difficult because of the design of
the hip socket. Try lifting your leg high to the
side, and you will see what I mean. Rotating the
whole leg through 90 degrees in the hip socket
helps solve this problem because the normal
relationship between the two halves of the hip

16

joint alters so that natural obstructions can be bypassed.

Since *turn out* extends the possibility of what dancers can do with their bodies, it has a very important effect on what we see on stage. It makes the dancers look sleek, elegant and poised, whether on the ground, or flying through the air. *Turning out* stops them tripping themselves up as they dance and is one of the most important ingredients of the classical line.

Dancers' muscles develop differently because of their highly specialized training. Their well developed thigh and calf muscles come from constant exercise like lifting the legs and *pliés*.

17

Warming Up Keeping the legs *turned out* requires great physical effort, and before class even begins, dancers will do a few preliminary warming up exercises. *'Frogs'* is a very effective exercise for loosening the legs in the hip sockets. While the dancers sit or lie on the floor their legs are not bearing the weight of the body, and can be eased slowly and naturally outward within the hip socket. Dancers who are loose enough to sit or lie in *frogs* without undue strain are said to be

'flat turned out', and for them *frogs* can even become a rather comfortable way of sitting! Like all dancers however, they will need to exercise constantly to maintain this *turn out* while moving.

Warming up alone before class, or a performance, is such an integral part of the dancer's life that it inspired Jerome Robbins to create his own version of the ballet, AFTERNOON OF A FAUN. On the stage, two dancers – a boy and a

girl – face the audience which becomes for them the mirrored wall of an empty classroom. They are so absorbed in their own reflections that they only gradually become aware of each other's presence. The ballet gives us a glimpse of the dedication and self-absorption that dancers need in order to succeed in a very tough profession. Dancers are of necessity, young people who will reach their peak, physically and artistically, by the age of 30. But though their physical powers tend to decline, great artistry can keep them dancing for many years.

Retired dancers often make very good teachers. Their great experience gives them an insight into the younger dancer's individual needs, and their memory of rôles that they have danced is very important when ballets are revived.

PART 1: THE CLASS

Introduction   Class is the daily ritual shared by all members of the company, from the most junior member of the *corps de ballet* to the most experienced soloist. It is divided into two parts, *the barre* and *center work*. Here we see some of the wide variety of stretching exercises that they do before and during class.

Any dancer soon discovers exercises which will show him the parts of the body that have suffered most during the previous evening's performance, and will need most attention in class before they begin to move freely again. These exercises will also help prevent further injuries. Stretching and warming up at intervals during a long working day, the dancer can work on his own for once and concentrate his mind on the tasks ahead.

THE BARRE

Introduction   The ballet mistress and the pianist have arrived. The dancers take their places and class begins, as always, with exercises at the *barre*. In a big class, extra *barres* will be carried to the middle of the room to give the dancers plenty of space.

Exercises at the *barre* are very important because as well as warming up the muscles they are designed to increase speed and precision of footwork, to prepare for jumps and turns, and to increase flexibility and strength in the spine. They also improve balance and increase the freedom of the legs and arms to move easily in their sockets. Great emphasis is laid on developing *turn out* and coordination. In the following pages we see a small sample of *barre* work.

A good pianist gives a cheerful atmosphere to the class and knows a hundred different pieces to suit the rhythms of all the exercises.

The very first exercise at the *barre* is always *pliés*. By this time, the dancers hope to be in a composed, if sleepy, frame of mind. Moving slowly up and down, occasionally checking their position in the mirror, they search for the center of balance within their bodies which every dancer must find at the beginning of the working day.

25

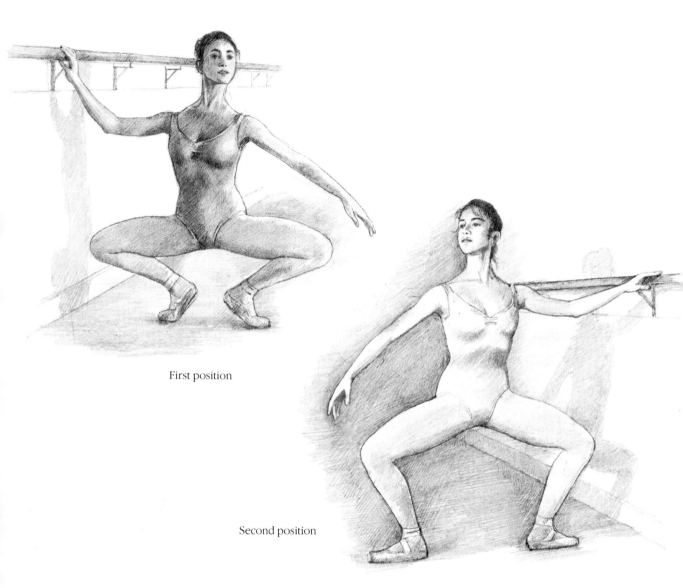

First position

Second position

Pliés   The fluid rise and fall of *pliés,* as they gently warm the leg muscles and the hip sockets, is the basis of all coordinated balletic movement. There are two types: the *grand plié* and the *demi-plié.* The *demi-plié* in the *fifth position* on the right hand page, is used constantly in jumps where its spring-like quality is vital for take off, and its cushioning effect for landing.

The *plié* is also very important in developing the flow of movement across the stage which is so characteristic of classical ballet. This flow is the dance equivalent of a melodic line in music, where isolated notes are woven into a musical phrase. Like other exercises at the *barre, pliés* are done in all five positions to practice the action of the legs to the front, back and sides.

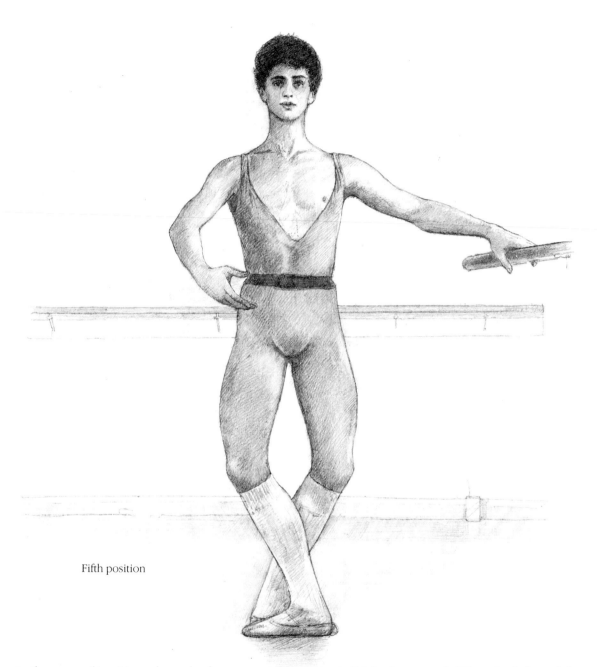

Fifth position

In the *second position* where the feet are quite far apart, the tendons in the legs are not very stretched, and the dancer can *plié* all the way down with her feet flat on the ground. In the middle drawing, she is still on her way down. On the previous page almost everyone is in a full *grand plié*. In the *grand plié* on the left, and the *demi plié* on the right (where the feet are closer together) the dancers can go down only so far before they allow their heels to lift gently from the floor, but they do try and keep them down as long as possible.

Grand Battement This exercise is designed to loosen the hips and hamstrings by throwing the leg as high as possible into the air. Like other *barre* exercises, *grands battements* are done to the front, the side and the back, and with both legs so that the dancer can develop an equal ability on either side of the body. Good *turn out* is particularly useful for high *battements* to the side, which the construction of the hip socket would otherwise make very difficult. *Grands battements* pass through one of the *tendu* positions which can also be seen in the drawing. *Tendus* are always done in class as an exercise in their own right, and the dancers concentrate on pointing and extending the leg to improve its line.

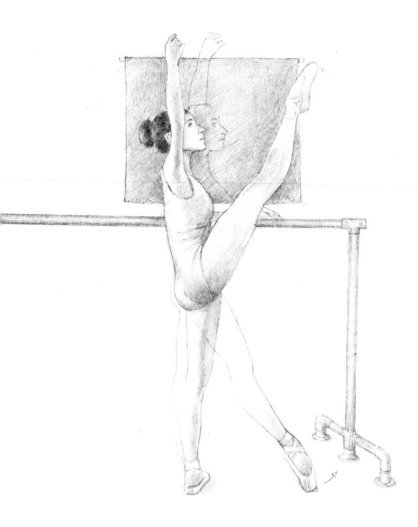

Increasingly, modern choreographers working in the classical style ask dancers to hold their legs in high positions. Since the same dancers also perform rôles in more traditional ballets, this has had an influence on their style as well. Classical ballet continues to evolve, and these innovations are always welcome when they do not go against the spirit of the dance. The photograph shows a modern use of a very high leg position from an American production of DON QUIXOTE, a traditional ballet.

Grands battements are impressive but actually need less strength and control than a slow unfolding *développé* ending up in the same position (pp. 127, 133).

Battement Fondu and Fouetté of Adage

The graceful linking of slow movements and jumps in classical ballet which give it its seamless romantic quality comes from the use of *fondu*. *Fondu* literally means 'to melt', and is really a *plié* on one leg. The *fondu* and the *plié* can be thought of, in more senses than one, as two of the mainsprings of ballet.

The *battement fondu* in the upper row of drawings shows something of the quality the dancer is looking for. She *fondus* with her supporting leg while bending her other leg inwards simultaneously. Both legs then unfold and straighten out in one fluid and controlled movement.

In the lower pair of drawings, the movement continues with a rotation of the body about the supporting leg. The dancer keeps her raised foot at the same height in the air, and maintains her *turn out* at the same time. This rotation is called a *fouetté of adage,* which means a 'slow, whipping turn'. In the *grand pas de deux* from THE SLEEPING BEAUTY (p. 126) you can see a similar movement, where this whipping round of the hips is done quickly for dramatic effect.

Look at the seven drawings again, and imagine the dancer's body slowly folding and unfolding in the *fondu,* and continuing in a slow and graceful rotation of the body ending in an *arabesque fondue,* as one continuous chain of movement. This is a small example of the language of classical choreography.

CENTER WORK

Introduction   At the end of *barre* work, there are more stretching and relaxing exercises to loosen the back and the muscles in other parts of the body which have worked hard in the previous three-quarters of an hour. If there are *barres* in the middle of the room, they are carried to one side. From now on all exercises will be done without their support.

Because these *center* exercises derive from classical choreography, they appear similar to what we will eventually see on stage. The combinations of steps, which become more difficult as the class goes on, are arranged by the ballet master or mistress to stimulate and test the dancers, and prepare their bodies for the greater demands of the choreographer. Choreography

is not merely the rearranging of well-known steps. On the contrary, creating new ballets also means creating new kinds of movement, which may in their turn inspire new exercises.

Center work can be divided into three broad sections: *Adage* which consists of slow sustained movements and *pirouettes*; *Petit Allegro* which is concerned with linking steps and small jumps

and finally *Grand Allegro* with its big leaps and turns. Above, the company is practicing a slow *adage* movement facing the right hand corner of the stage. When on tour, companies frequently do their classes and rehearsals on stage because of lack of space.

Alignments   Exercises in the center often start and finish facing diagonally across the room. This is true of the later jumps and turns as well as the early slow movements done on the spot. The direction the dancers face, known as their *alignment,* is another very important element of the classical style because it controls the outline of the body which the audience sees. If all movements were done facing the front, they might become monotonous. Notice how facing the right-hand corner of the stage, or facing the left-hand corner, changes the outline of the two dancers' bodies. These different shapes show two of the most basic *alignments* of the body. They are the open position, known as *effacé,* (or *ouvert,* meaning 'opened up') and the more compact position with the leg crossing behind or in front of the body, known as *croisé* (crossed). In either case, the hips face one corner of the stage. Standing on the other leg, but facing

34

in the same direction, would change the *effacé* to *croisé* and the *croisé* to *effacé*.

Dancers must take care to use correct *alignment* on stage, because the beauty of the body's shape in different positions depends as much on the space we see between the limbs, as on the correctness of the position itself. If the wrong parts of the body are hidden, then the purity of line that the spectator sees will be lost.

To understand how *alignment* is maintained

you have to imagine, as dancers do before it becomes second nature, that they are standing in the middle of a square which moves around with them. Invisible lines are drawn diagonally and at right angles through its center to mark the different *alignments*. As long as the dancer is standing correctly within the box, keeping the front of the box parallel with the front of the stage, he will always know the exact angle of his body in relation to the audience.

Alignments: Croisé to Effacé

The dancer is standing on one leg and moving the other leg from front to back. She goes from *croisé devant* (crossed in front) to *effacé derrière* (open behind). These are the technical names of the positions, which we can imagine being linked by slow, continuous movements. See how many positions the dancer goes through, and notice how the shape of the body changes too. We see her as if we are sitting in the center of the front row of the dress circle.

Starting on the extreme right, the dancer stands in an *extension croisé devant,* the raised leg pointing in front of the supporting leg. Then

slowly bending the knee, she stands in an *attitude croisée devant*. She lowers her leg, keeping it well turned out and extended, in a *tendu croisé devant*. Slowly the leg moves back becoming a *tendu effacé derrière,* also known as an *arabesque à terre* (or *arabesque* with the toe on the ground). Then as her leg moves up, bending again at the knee, the position becomes an *attitude effacée derrière,* and finally her leg straightens out, and she is in an *arabesque*.

Compared to the drawings, the *tendu croisé devant* from George Balanchine's BALLET IMPERIAL (see inset) shows an exaggerated use of *alignment* in the upper part of the body.

37

Alignments: Efface to Croisé

The dancer is aligned along the other diagonal. This time, moving the raised leg from front to back, he goes from *effacé* to *croisée*. Starting with an open *extension effacé devant*, he bends his leg slightly, transforming it into an *attitude effacée devant,* followed by a *tendu effacé devant*. As his leg moves through to the back, the first position he goes through, as he extends and points his foot, is a *tendu croisé derrière,* followed by an *attitude croisée derrière* as he raises and slightly bends his leg. Then he opens his leg out into an *arabesque.*

For a correct *alignment* to be of any use, the dancer's position in that *alignment* must be perfect. So the idea of *alignment* is not introduced to young dancers until they begin to understand the importance of the classical line. The photograph shows a *tendu croisé derrière* from NAPOLI, the ballet choreographed by August Bournonville.

Alignments: Écarté This is another diagonal *alignment* of the body, but it has a quite different feel from *croisée* and *effacé* because here the body is flattened on the diagonal. *Écarté* means 'thrown wide apart', and is an extension of the *second position,* where legs and arms open out directly to the side. When a dancer is in *écarté* to the front, she tilts her head towards her raised arm as in the pictures on the left-hand page.

When in *écarté* to the back she looks down the line of her lowered arm. Because of the angle at which we see her, the raised leg looks very long. This makes a dramatic shape if held long enough for the audience to appreciate the effect. In the two inset examples of *écarté* from THE SLEEPING BEAUTY, Florestan and one of his sisters *développé* in *écarté devant* and Aurora is supported in *écarté derrière* by one of her suitors.

Arabesque   In its many forms and moods the *arabesque* is seen and recognized more often than any other shape of the body in classical ballet. We see it at its most exuberant in the *first arabesque* position on *pointe,* and in its male equivalent, on *half-pointe* as above. It is used in lifts, jumps, turns, *promenades* and *pirouettes,* and the *pas de deux*. To form an *arabesque,* one leg is raised and extended behind the body and a variety of shapes of the arms is used to harmonize with its long, extended line. A great artist is able to give a different emotional color to each *arabesque* by subtle variations of height and carriage of the arms and legs.

The fashion for very high *arabesques* is quite recent. Those dancers who concentrate only on the height of the leg at the expense of all else, risk distorting the lovely calm effect of this position.

The terms *first*, *second* and *third arabesque* are used for the different arm positions that go with the raised leg. In different countries the positions themselves may vary as well as the way of naming them, but shown here and on the following pages are those most commonly used.

First Arabesque   This is the *first arabesque.* In the photograph on the left, we see an example on *pointe,* from The Black Swan *pas de deux.* The feeling is electric, full of life and spirit. By contrast, the *first arabesque* on the flat of the foot has a more serene and regal air. It feels poised and open. It is very important in the *arabesque* to keep the hips as square as possible facing forwards, and to avoid the natural tendency of the *arabesque* leg to pull the pelvis upwards. At the same time, *turn out* must be maintained. The *arabesque* leg, in both pictures, is rotated in the hip socket causing the heel to turn away from us.

First Arabesque   The photograph shows a moment of gentle symmetry from Les Sylphides, a ballet choreographed by Mikhail Fokine to music by Frederick Chopin. The costumes are the long tutus of the Romantic Period which reveal little of the body, except the arms, ankles and feet.

In the drawing, three girls rehearse the same moment from the ballet. The two outer girls stand in yet another example of the *first arabesque* position.

Classical choreographers use the *arabesque* in all its various forms again and again, because of its beautiful shape and its power to suggest a range of human emotions.

The way that the two outer girls are holding their arms so that they drop slightly over the leg is not strictly correct, and has been done to match the photograph. Today, video films are often used to help in restaging ballets, but they are not really a good substitute for the memory of an intelligent soloist who performed in an earlier production. There is always the risk that without personal guidance, dancers will imitate the style of another dancer, or worse still, repeat mistakes which have become fixed forever on film.

Second Arabesque The position of the arms seen in the *first arabesque* has been reversed. The arm nearest us now points forward, extending the long line of the leg on the same side of the body, instead of being held above it and parallel as before. The crossed line of the arms causes the dancer's upper back to turn very slightly towards us, revealing the shoulders, and adds a feeling of yearning, of physical and emotional tension. Later on (pp. 90, 91) there are two examples of this *arabesque* done as a *grand jeté*.

Third Arabesque   Both arms reach forward in a combination of the *first* and *second arabesque* positions. With no arm behind to counterbalance the upper part of the body, this position gives a feeling of reaching forward, of searching. Like all the *arabesques* and other positions, the *third arabesque* is seen as one link in a continuous chain of movement. To dancers, every momentary position that the body passes through requires the same attention, but to the spectator, certain beautiful shapes, like the *arabesque,* stay longer in the memory than others, particularly when seen as a final pose on *pointe* after a dazzling solo.

Arabesque Fondue   The *fondu* always has a soft, yielding and expressive quality. It also prepares the dancer to continue into some other movement. Sometimes, as a choreographic motif, the *fondu* may be seen as a series of little hops or jumps; in Swan Lake, Odette, the Prince and the swans all do this at different times.

In the photograph from Act 1 of Swan Lake, Anthony Dowell shows just how much feeling can be expressed by perfect line in a *fondu*. The

bend at the knee lowers the whole body, and concentrates the eye even more on the long line of the *arabesque*. At the same time, there is no feeling of a static pose. The great sculptor, Auguste Rodin, who said that for sculpture to have life it must give 'the illusion of movement in progress', would surely have been inspired by Dowell as he was by Nijinsky.

Arabesque Penchée   This is a tilted *arabesque* where the whole body leans forward and is counterbalanced by the raised leg.

In this *penché* from GISELLE the dancer is taking the part of a Wili. Wilis are the spirits of young girls who have died of broken hearts after being

deserted by their fiancés, and quite appropriately she folds her arms gently in front of her in a gesture symbolizing death and resignation. The hips should be kept square, but the long tutu will make any error slightly less obvious!

This second example of an *arabesque penchée* is in the *first arabesque* position. The photograph shows the entire *corps de ballet* in La Bayadère, which was one of Marius Petipa's most successful ballets in Russia at the end of the nineteenth century. It was rarely seen in the West in its complete form until it was restaged for the American Ballet Theatre by Natalia Makarova.

It is also famous for the incredibly dramatic effect when 32 members of the *corps de ballet* enter in a series of high *arabesques fondues*, coming down a long incline. The *corps de ballet* both here and in Swan Lake are often asked to stand on one leg for long periods of time as a backdrop to the soloists. This can become excruciatingly painful, and to make matters worse, they will then be expected to spring into action, even though cramp may have set in. If you are fortunate enough to watch a performance of either of these ballets from the wings, then you may be surprised by the muffled mutterings coming from some of the dancers.

55

Attitude After the *arabesque,* the second most frequently seen shape in the répertoire of classical positions is probably the *attitude.* The *attitude* gives a feeling of enclosing space because of the wrapped-around quality of the raised leg which is bent at the knee (in front or behind) and is quite different from the *arabesque's* long, harmonious extended line. It is its sculptural quality that makes the *attitude* so interesting in turns where it presents a constantly changing silhouette.

Like the *arabesque* it has its own special beauty and is also used in jumps, lifts, *promenades* and *pirouettes.* It is often used as a midway position

in slow unfolding movements, and in the *pas de deux* section there are two examples of this where the ballerina balances briefly on *pointe* in *attitude,* and then, thrillingly, opens out into an *arabesque* (pp. 114, 124).

In the inset from THE SLEEPING BEAUTY we see the *attitude croisée derrière,* (or attitude crossed

behind). The *attitude effacée derrière* (opened up, behind) on the right looks a little ungainly on the flat foot but on *pointe* it changes completely and can be a stunningly beautiful pose.

Attitude Effacée Derrière   These two
pictures both show variations of the *attitude
effacée derrière* but this time we see the dancer
from the back. Here we can see just how
expressive the back in an *attitude* can be. On the
left, the raised leg starts a lovely curved line
which leads our eye past her upraised face, along
her arm and beyond. On the right, the same line
leads us more directly to the face, which is turned
towards us.

Both of these *attitudes* are extremely difficult
to hold. Maintaining the height of the leg,
coupled with the slight rotation of the upper
back, requires strength, balance and control. The
spectator seldom realizes what is necessary to
create such a lyrical effect.

58

59

60

Attitude Croisée Devant   The dancer
in this *attitude croisée devant* stands confidently
on *pointe,* her leg crossed and bent at the knee in
front of her body. The lifted arms complement
the high position of the leg, and the shape of the
tutu. In the performance photograph taken from
the end of a sparkling solo from THE SLEEPING
BEAUTY, she seems to be saying 'What did you
think of that'. Needless to say, this is usually
accompanied by an enthusiastic response from
the audience.

61

Pointe Work   The image of a dancer
standing on *pointe,* is a symbol of ballet and is
seen in no other form of dance. It lengthens the
classical and romantic line and was first used by
Marie Taglioni in LA SYLPHIDE to give the
impression of a sylph skimming along the
ground. There is a strong, steely quality
underneath its soft romanticism which can be
used for dramatic effect.

Pointe work should never be attempted by
young dancers before the age of 12 because it
puts tremendous pressure and strain on the feet
and can easily distort them as the bones are not
yet fully grown. For rehearsals and for *pointe*
work later in the class, dancers take off the
battered and softened *pointe* shoes they have
been wearing, and change into harder ones.
Even though every dancer has shoes especially

made by hand to fit her feet, brand new ones will first be banged on the floor or trampled on, to soften them up a bit.

In the drawing, the dancers are standing on *pointe* in three of the *basic positions*. On the left in the background, one girl stands with her feet flat on the ground, while the other leans on the *barre* testing her shoes. Both are in the *second position*. In the foreground, another dancer standing next to her *pas de deux* partner flexes her feet in a turned in position done as an exercise, but not often seen on stage. Behind her, a dancer stands in the streamlined *fifth position* on *pointe* which we will see on *bourées* in the following pages. The photograph from George Balanchine's Apollo is a fine example of the *fourth position* on *pointe*.

Bourrées   During the *adage* section of class,
dancers practice *arabesques, attitudes,* and other
positions, slowly transforming the body's outline
from one position to another in different
alignments. As class progresses, different types
of movement are added, turning them into steps,
jumps or turns. *Bourrées* are an exciting
transformation of the *fifth position* on *pointe,* a
way of gliding smoothly across or around the
stage. The feet make hundreds of tiny steps
which give a brilliant shimmering appearance to
the legs.

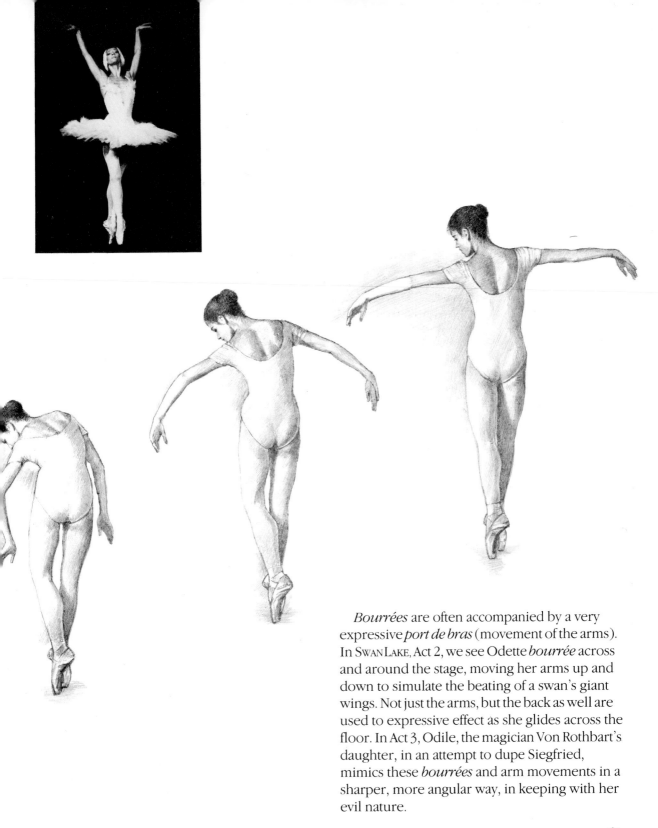

Bourrées are often accompanied by a very expressive *port de bras* (movement of the arms). In SWAN LAKE, Act 2, we see Odette *bourrée* across and around the stage, moving her arms up and down to simulate the beating of a swan's giant wings. Not just the arms, but the back as well are used to expressive effect as she glides across the floor. In Act 3, Odile, the magician Von Rothbart's daughter, in an attempt to dupe Siegfried, mimics these *bourrées* and arm movements in a sharper, more angular way, in keeping with her evil nature.

65

Bourrées are done on the spot as well as moving across the stage, and here the shimmering of the legs may be even more obvious. In these drawings, we see part of a turn of the body, combined with another expressive *port de bras* which comes from the famous Rose Adagio from THE SLEEPING BEAUTY, Act 1.

Natalia Makarova has described the way the arms and back should be used. It is not just a question of waving the arms up and down, slowly or quickly. Arms and back should be able to show a range of emotions from light-heartedness to sorrow. This will come more naturally to a dancer with an expressive and intuitive nature, and slender, mobile and graceful arms.

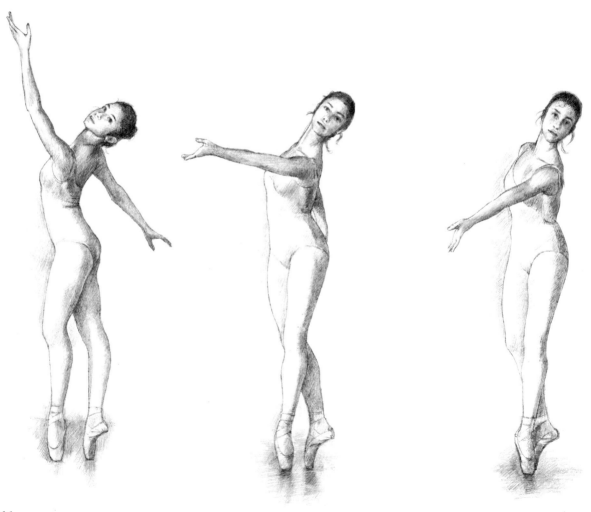

Pirouette   One of the most exciting endings
to a solo is a series of effortless *pirouettes*.
Because there is always an element of risk
involved, even the most experienced dancers
worry about *pirouettes* and practice them every
day in class. *Pirouettes* make an impressive
display when they come off perfectly, but off-
balance *pirouettes* are impossible to hide.

Some dancers are fortunate enough to have a
natural ability to balance and turn well. For them,
as well as for dancers who do not mind falling
over occasionally, *pirouettes* can be fun.

In the three rows of dancers on the left-hand
page, you can see part of the preparation for a
pirouette on *half-pointe* from the *fourth position*.

At first, they *tendu* to the *second position,* then
they bring the working foot behind and *demi-plié*
in the *fourth position.* Pushing away from the
floor, they turn swiftly into the *pirouette* with a
whipping action of the head, while pulling the
working leg up into the *retiré* position.

Provided the body is perfectly balanced, and
turns as a single unit after this initial push-off, the
dancer gets enough momentum to keep the
body turning a number of times simply by
whipping the head around. This is known as
'spotting', because the dancer focuses on one
spot in the room as long as possible before
whipping the head back to the same spot again.

69

Pirouette on Pointe   The preparation for a *pirouette* on *pointe* is exactly the same as the preparation for the *pirouette* on *half-pointe* on the previous page, except that the dancer rises quickly onto full *pointe* at the moment of push-off. In these drawings, we imagine that the dancer has started turning on *pointe* and makes her last complete turn before returning to the

fourth position with her arms extended forward in a firm and open position called *demi-bras*.

While turning, the dancer concentrates on a number of different things all at the same time. She must hold her stomach in, keeping her *working leg* well *turned out* while the muscles in the *supporting leg* must be well 'pulled up'. She must maintain the position of the arms, and

70

make sure that her foot does not slip out from its position next to the knee and 'over cross' it. She must keep the body taut, but not too rigid while she turns. All this helps her maintain the imaginary axis running from the top of her head, down through her spine, through her leg and toe and into the ground.

Spotting, and turning in rhythm with the music, keeps the *pirouette* going and helps the dancer know when and where to stop. The finish, when it comes, must be as strong, clear and decisive as the turn itself, especially as the dancer may feel slightly dizzy and must avoid any tendency to wobble.

Pirouette in Attitude   Although *pirouettes* in *retiré* (with one toe drawn up to the knee) can be done from almost any position, *pirouettes* in *attitude* and in *arabesque* usually start from the firm, wide platform of the *fourth position* with the back leg straightened out. This allows more initial impetus, as the weight of the raised leg tends to pull the dancer off balance.

In the four drawings above, the dancer has already pushed off, and is turning on *pointe* with her arms raised in the *fifth position*. In the second drawing she passes through an *attitude croisée derrière*. In the third drawing another three-quarter turn takes her to *attitude éffacée derrière,* and she finishes in *attitude croisée derrière* again. As the dancer turns, you can see the sculptural

qualities of the *attitude,* at every stage.

    Pirouettes in different positions, like the *attitude* and the arabesque, give the choreographer plenty of choice when creating groups of steps. The finishing position, standing on the flat of one foot, is much more difficult than the *fourth position* finish of the earlier *pirouette.* Tremendous coordination and balance are

needed to arch the back and the *attitude* leg towards each other while standing on one leg. The position of the open arms, apart from its pleasing shape, also acts as a sort of balancing pole.

Pirouette in Arabesque In these pages we see two *pirouettes* in *arabesque* chosen to show how a very different emotional quality can be achieved by using different positions of the arms and legs. This slow turning *pirouette* is often used in slow *adage* sequences because of its elegant and romantic line.

In the first drawing, the arms start in the *second position*. As the dancer slowly turns, they move upwards to the *fifth position*. Raising the

arms in the *fifth position* lengthens the long, curved *arabesque* line, and forms a moving frame for the head. In the third picture the dancer has deliberately raised his shoulder slightly, to show a common fault that spoils the feeling of space around the head. In a performance this may not really matter; the expressive line of the body, which is far more important, would stay in the memory longer than any small error.

The high leg in this *pirouette* gives it a more brilliant image, an impression of technical skill more than of emotion. Like the earlier turn it is done quite slowly, but the higher leg gives it a feeling of sailing around the center point. It needs tremendous strength to hold the hips completely square and level (see the first drawing on the right) while holding the *working*

leg out at right angles to the body. Even the best dancers will tend to displace their hips slightly (see last drawing) due to the effort of turning with the leg in this position. Even though the dancer is looking at herself in the mirror, she may be turning too fast to see what is going wrong. The teacher will notice though, and will come over and correct her.

PETIT ALLEGRO

Introduction   After practicing *pirouettes* the dancers move on to the next important part of the class, called *petit allegro*, where they jump for the first time. The first jumps are quite small, taking off and landing on two feet. Typical is the *échappé* on the left hand side of the page which is a jumped version of the *second position*. To perform the *échappé,* they *demi-plié* in the *fifth*

position, *échappé* (escape) their legs to the *second position* in the air, as in the drawing, and land on the ground with their feet apart in the *second position*. Then they make another jump which finishes back in the *fifth position*. It is very important for the dancers to concentrate on the upwards spring, pointing their feet downwards as they jump, as slack feet spoil the thrusting line

of the leg. *Échappés* are also done in the *fourth position* with one leg behind the other. There are many similar exercises such as *changements de pieds* where the dancers spring up and change the position of the feet, before landing again in the *fifth position*. All these little jumps help warm up the legs for the bigger jumps and *entrechats* later on.

In the drawing on the right, the dancers are seen in the *retiré sauté*. The *retiré* position is used in all sorts of disguises; in *pirouettes,* and in turns and jumps in the air; as part of many *adage* steps (pp. 124, 132), and in some of the other jumps we are about to see like the *pas de chat* and the *ballotté*.

79

Pas de Chat   The *pas de chat* (or step of the cat) involves more than one movement of the legs and travels a certain distance through the air. Its best known use is probably in the dance of the cats (Puss in Boots and the White Cat) in Act 3 of THE SLEEPING BEAUTY. The drawings may give the impression that the *pas de chat* consists of a series of poses; in fact it is one light, fast and snappy movement. It does not require great strength and is one of the first jumps that children learn to do, both because the action of leaping off one foot and chasing it with the other comes naturally to them, but also because they find the idea of the cat appealing.

The *pas de chat* is very common and is seen in many different contexts; in the dance of the four little swans from SWAN LAKE, and here in LA SYLPHIDE where we see the Scottish hero, James, perform this step in a kilt.

Assemblé   In this jump the two feet are brought together or 'assembled' in the air before the dancer lands on the ground. It is done in all directions on stage either as a small or as a very large jump and is frequently done with the legs beating together in the air before landing. It is never a truly virtuoso step unless done as a very big *beaten* jump. It can also be performed while turning in the air.

Its main use is as one of the most common

linking steps in a dance, as it is a convenient way of moving from a step which ends on one foot, to another which starts on two feet from a *demi-plié*. Dancers learn to do *assemblés* in class, jumping up and down on the spot. The *assemblé* in the

drawings is the kind more usually seen on stage, which travels a certain distance in the air. The forward lean of the dancer's body emphasizes the feeling of flight.

Ballotté   This is a light-hearted, springy step. The legs toss backwards and forwards, the body leaning forwards and backwards with each change of weight in order to counterbalance them. The *ballotté* is not attempted until the dancer is at an advanced level because it takes great strength in the spine and feet as well as good balance. Any jumping step needs *elevation*, or the ability to get off the ground, but for *petit allegro* steps like the *ballotté* there is a special quality called *ballon*. *Ballon* literally means 'bounce' and is an easy bounding and rebounding from the stage; imagine a rubber ball being bounced against the floor and you will see how essential it is for keeping the momentum going in any series of small jumps like the *ballotté*. Giselle is a ballet where the use of *ballottés* is very obvious.

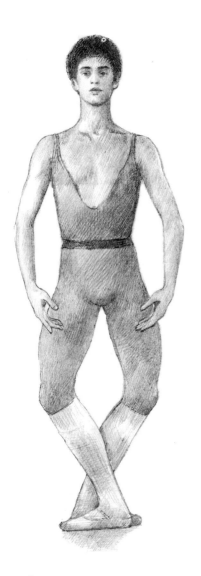

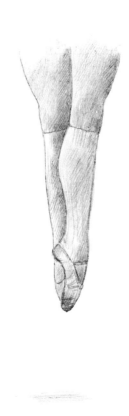

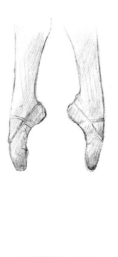

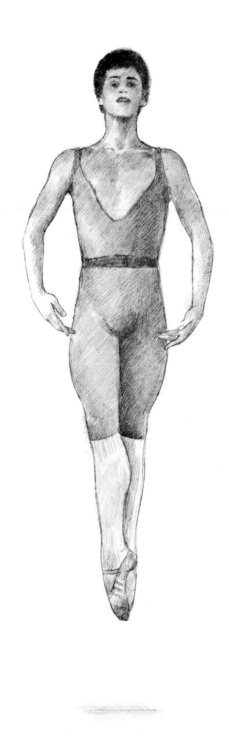

Entrechat One of the most exciting steps in ballet is when dancers leap straight up in the air and beat their feet together, in front and behind, a number of times before landing. The whole leg crosses and recrosses, not just the lower half. The example shown here is one of the simplest as the feet have only changed twice before landing. In *grand allegro* the dancers will do *entrechats six* where the feet cross over three times.

Done in a series, *entrechats* have a virile brilliant quality although they are done not only by men, but also by girls. They are often combined with other steps and jumps. Serge Lifar maintained that sparkling beats are easier to achieve if the dancer is slightly bow-legged, since his feet do not have to travel so far to cross and uncross.

GRAND ALLEGRO

Introduction   The climax of the class is *grand allegro*. The dancers are fully warmed up and ready to practice steps of virtuosity: spectacular leaps, turns in the air, and high beaten steps. To stimulate their interest, and test them to the full, the ballet master arranges *enchâinements* (chains of steps) which are just like parts of the finished ballet they will perform later on the stage.

Classical ballet demands that men in particular, should be able to perform steps of *grand élévation* with apparent ease, as they will need these movements for solo variations. Although girls do many of the same steps and jumps, in a high jump like the *grand jeté in attitude* seen above; for example, boys tend to

concentrate on the height of the jump while girls emphasize *extension* of the legs. In order to have enough room when practicing travelling steps, dancers go across the classroom from corner to corner in small groups.

By the end of class, the calm, unhurried pace of those first *pliés* has been replaced by an atmosphere similar to a Turkish bath. On stage that night, there will be no hint of effort or strain, but now the great crashing noise of eight simultaneous landings from a high jump may be followed by muffled curses, as one of the dancers limps away.

Grand Jeté in Second Arabesque

The *grand jeté* is one of the highest, and for the spectator, one of the most exciting jumps in classical ballet. It should be smooth and effortless, seeming to defy the laws of gravity. To produce this effect, the dancer should appear to soar through the air and land as lightly as possible. To do this requires years of training. *Turn out* and complete control of the body's shape in the air must be maintained throughout.

Here are two extended versions of the *second arabesque* position, The crossed line of the legs

90

and body, as the dancer on the left jumps
diagonally towards us, gives a bright exuberant
feeling. On the right we see the same jump done
with the legs in the *effacé* rather than the *croisé
alignment* and the feeling is quite different. The
slight curve of the upper back adds to the effect

of the more romantic curving line running from
her toe to her upstretched hand.

Americans and Russians are noted for the
excitement and bravura of their travelling steps
and jumps, a direct result of the freedom that
their larger stages gives them.

Grand Jeté in Third Arabesque   The photograph shows Merrill Ashley of the New York City Ballet in George Balanchine's SYMPHONY IN C executing a *grand jeté* with her arms in the *third arabesque* position. Choreographers choose different positions in *grands jetés* to provide variety, and to suit the different moods of the music. Balanchine uses this *grand jeté* to suit one of the extrovert moments of the *allegro vivace*.

The dancers in the two pictures above have anatomically different types of leg. The dancer on the left has straight legs, and the one on the right has slightly 'swayback' legs which have a more undulating outline. In each case however the back leg looks completely straight because it is *turned out* fully towards us. Any young dancer will look at these two pictures with a mixture of admiration and perhaps just a hint of jealousy.

Flick Jeté   This very different *jeté* is typical of the new classical style. It is part of a trend towards more athleticism and gymnastic ability without sacrificing too much of the expressiveness of the older tradition.

A jump like this needs daring and attack, a lot of flexibility, and use of the back. The backward bend with the arms in the *fifth position* gives a feeling of controlled abandon, very different from the ethereal quality of the romantic and

94

classical ballets.
    The photograph shows Svetlana Beriosova,
rehearsing a moment from Balanchine's APOLLO.
Note her superb line and *turn out*.

Cabriole Derrière   The *cabriole* is very common in classical ballet and is very impressive and exciting when done as a big jump. The dancer jumps, *beats* his legs together in front or behind before landing again. In the drawing we see a *cabriole derrière* where the body makes an elegant curving line. In preparation for this *cabriole,* the dancer *fondus* in the *first arabesque position,* and leaps upwards, bringing the *fondu* leg up to *beat* against the *arabesque* leg, before returning to the ground in the *first arabesque position* again. The photograph from Sir Frederick Ashton's THE TWO PIGEONS shows a splendid *cabriole derrière*. A long line runs down in an elegant curve from the upraised hand to the feet, which are slightly blurred as they *beat* behind.

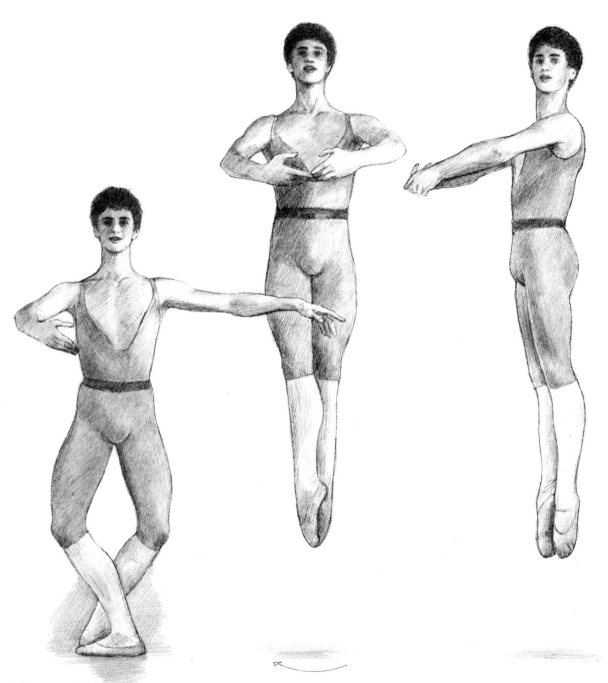

Tour en L'Air   A spectacular jump in which the dancer leaps directly upwards and turns one, two or three times before landing. It is seen very frequently as part of a chain of steps, or as the final flourish in a solo.

In the example here, we show only one turn for simplicity. Starting from a *demi-plié* in the *fifth position,* the dancer springs from the floor, turning rapidly with the body absolutely firm and straight. If there is a wobble on landing the whole

98

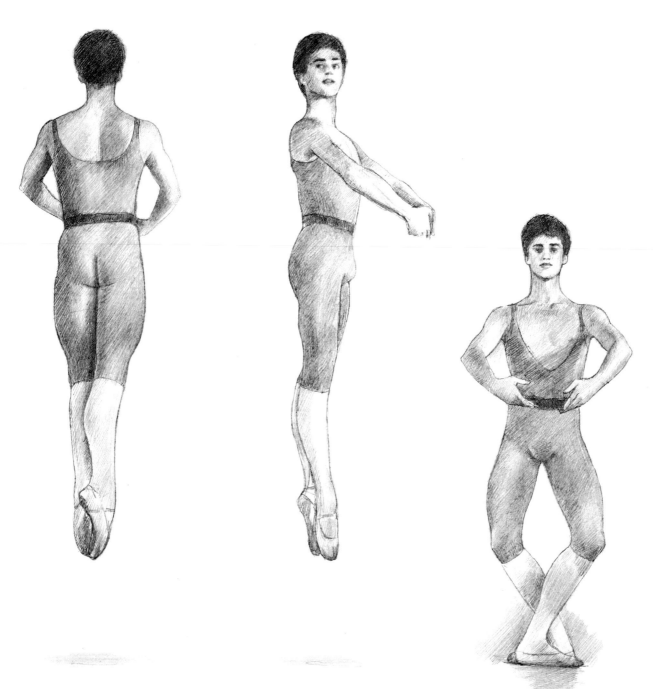

effect is spoilt. At some point during the second turn in the air, the dancer changes feet. When he does this is entirely up to him, but as a result, he always lands with his feet crossed the other way round.

When done as the climax to a variation, the *tour en l'air* often finishes dramatically on one knee, or the dancer may *relevé* from the finishing *plié,* into an elegant *fifth position* with his arms raised above his head.

Brisé Volé   This virtuso step requires considerable strength and *ballon* and is best known from the Bluebird variation of THE SLEEPING BEAUTY, where the Bluebird does a series of them across the stage. The *brisé* is a travelling jump, forwards or backwards, with a *beat*. The *brisés volés* in the Bluebird variation alternate both types of *brisé* with a bird-like *port de bras,* and this, combined with the forward and backward swaying of the body and the beating of

the feet, gives an impression of flight.

For the *brisé volé* to be effective, the spectator must see sparkling and clearly defined *beats* of the whole leg, with both legs fully stretched. Arching the body well forward, and then well backwards, with soft landings and springy rebounds in between, is vital. The momentum must be kept going, and any jarring of the step will spoil it, and bring the dancer to a halt.

Temps de Poisson   Like the *fish dive* this is one of the steps in classical ballet where the body is supposed to take on the form of a fish. In this case it is meant to imitate the salmon's elegant curve as it leaps proudly up a series of waterfalls on its way to the spawning ground. It can be done in a backwards or forwards series, when the dancer may land on one foot, then do an *assemblé* to get back into the *fifth position,* before leaping again. Alternatively *temps de poisson* can be done one after the other, by landing in a *demi-plié* in the *fifth position,* and then springing straight up into another *temps de poisson,* and so on.

Needless to say this jump is far more difficult than it looks; the elegant curve must come from arching the whole body. Teachers will always stress the importance of avoiding a bend at the knees, which might seem a short cut but will certainly not fool an expert audience. The *temps de poisson* is yet another use of the *fifth position.*

Barrel Turn   There are many jumps for male dancers that go around the stage. One of the most common of these is the *coupe jeté en tournant* known as the *barrel turn*. It looks like a spiralling chain of *grands jetés* in *attitude*.

Each curving jump is followed by a quick turn on the ground which incorporates the landing of the previous jump, and the take off for the next jump together with a quick change of feet (the *coupé*) which the spectator is unlikely to be able to see. These turns are extremely exciting to watch, especially if the dancer has good *elevation*.

The *barrel turn* is not difficult physically, but

104

requires various tricks of the trade which some dancers never master. Most important of these is leaning inwards, on the turns. This counteracts the tendency of the body to fly off to one side instead of carrying on around. Many Russian dancers including Nureyev, seen in full flight in Le Corsaire in the photograph, lean over so far that they are almost parallel with the floor, which is very spectacular. It is important to keep the turning rhythm going, to go down as low as possible when landing, and turning on the ground before leaping up again, as high as possible, into the next *jeté*.

PART II: REHEARSAL AND PAS DE DEUX

Introduction   At the end of the class the dancers will be exhausted, and after thanking their teacher by clapping enthusiastically, there will usually be a break for refreshment before the day's rehearsals begin. The company may well rehearse several different ballets on the same day if it is a touring company because the next program must be started while the current ballet is kept up to scratch. So some time during the day, *pas de deux* will be rehearsed.

Ballet enthusiasts are so used to seeing the male dancer as a brilliant solo artist, that they tend to underestimate the importance of his role as a partner in the classical and romantic *pas de deux*. This is partly because it is his job to concentrate the audience's attention on the ballerina while he extends the limits of all her solo steps; helps her float effortlessly over impossible distances in the supported *grand jeté*, make innumerable turns in supported *pirouettes* and *finger fouettés*, and supports her in *promenades*, and lifts.

In the *pas de deux,* the dancers must move as one body and must always seem to act under the same impulse. From the practical point of view, the ballerina needs a partner with whom she has an almost telepathic understanding and in whom she has complete trust. Otherwise her own dancing will be affected by a slight holding back, resulting from an unconscious fear of injury. All movement is a joint effort; a high lift would often be impossible without her discreet *plié* and push-off, added to her partner's effort. The *pas de deux* is a small drama at the heart of most ballets, and whether it is romantic, sad, light-hearted or aggressive, each dancer must contribute his or her share to their joint effort or risk a lifeless performance, and even a broken nose!

The photograph shows Anthony Dowell and Antoinette Sibley in Sir Frederick Ashton's production of CINDERELLA. He supports her in a variation of *third arabesque.* She could not possibly stand in this position by herself, since her center of balance is thrown in front of her feet. The forward reach of the arms always gives a feeling of yearning and the complementary shapes of their bodies, only adds to this impression.

In the photograph on the left, we see another moment from CINDERELLA. This time the ballerina stands on *pointe* and her partner gives her the barest possible support, as she leans lightly against his chest. He echoes the shape of her body with his own.

Many *grands pas de deux* represent moments from a love story, and the male partner strives to demonstrate his passion for her, while at the same time, showing off her beauty to best advantage to the audience. Sooner or later, some small gesture of hers will reassure him that his feelings are reciprocated. In this instance it is the very act of leaning against him, symbolizing trust and tenderness.

The second photograph is from Sir Kenneth MacMillan's bedroom *pas de deux* from his production of ROMEO AND JULIET. Here they dance a joyful celebration of what is to be their wedding night. This forbidden and tragic love affair with its brief marriage is more tempestuous, more violent in its passion than the lighter mood of CINDERELLA (as the photographs show).

Supported Attitude and Supported Arabesque   The drawing on the left shows a supported *attitude croisée derrière* and the drawing on the right shows a supported *first arabesque*. At its simplest, the support of the partner enables the ballerina to stand longer on *pointe* than she would normally be able to do unaided. As a development from these two positions, her partner can walk around her, turning her on *pointe* in a slow supported *pirouette* in *attitude* or in *arabesque*. This is known as a *promenade*.

The *attitude* on the left is also often seen as the finishing position of a series of supported *pirouettes*, see p.117. The boy must be very careful to keep all his steps at the same distance from his partner's foot, otherwise he will easily overbalance her.

Promenade in Attitude

A famous example of the *promenade in attitude* comes in the Rose Adagio from THE SLEEPING BEAUTY. Four princely suitors *promenade* Aurora in turn, each supporting her with his outstretched hand. Between each *promenade* she raises her other arm and balances on *pointe*. This *fifth position* of the arms is sometimes known as *'en couronne'* (like a crown) which is very appropriate in this context. At the end, she again raises her arm, balances, then as the music swells to a crescendo, opens out her arms and *attitude* leg into a

114

stunning *arabesque effacée* as seen in the last drawing.

The spectator may not realise that all this is extremely difficult. When she is supported at the waist (previous page) it would be relatively easy, but here the only contact is between their two hands. The dancers must really work well together, particularly since it is very easy for him to throw her off-balance. Not surprisingly, it is quite rare to see this *promenade* executed without a slight wobble at some point.

Finger Fouettés   In the supported *pirouette,* the dancer is able to push away from the floor but in the *finger fouetté,* she starts on *pointe* and the impetus for the turn comes mainly from pushing off from her partner's lower hand, and from the whipping round action of her raised leg. She starts by bringing her right leg up into *retiré,* then, bringing her leg straight out in front (first drawing) she whips it to the side and back into *retiré* again as she turns, lightly holding his middle finger directly above her head. With his support, she can turn many times like this.

Supported Pirouette   The girl's
preparation in this type of supported *pirouette* is
exactly the same as for the unsupported
pirouette. Her partner stands directly behind her,
with his hands lightly supporting her at the waist.
With his support she may do more turns than she
normally could unaided, because if she does get
slightly off balance, he can correct her
imperceptibly. The dancers must have a very
close understanding, because an unsympathetic
partner could easily ruin a perfectly good series
of *pirouettes* by being heavy-handed.

In this type of *pirouette,* she will finish in a
pose on *pointe* (see p.113) and her partner is
ready to support her at the waist. In other types
of *pirouette* where she starts on *pointe* (instead
of from a *fourth position*) her partner will start
her turning by feeding her waist through his
hands.

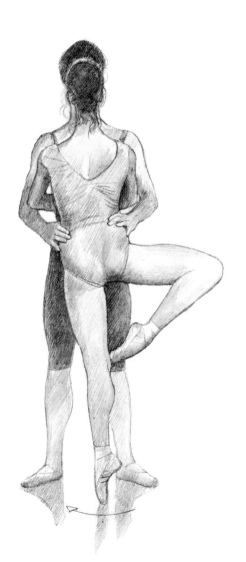

Fall In this supported fall from the White Swan *pas de deux* Siegfried lowers Odette so that she faces us. Her weight does not, in fact, rest on his thigh as it seems to in the pictures, so she needs to jam her back foot into the floor to stop herself from sliding away to the right. The position which she has to hold herself in at the full length of his arm, is the same *fifth position* that we saw in *pointe* work (p.62) and *bourrées* (p.64), except that here her body makes a beautiful curve, counterbalanced by his raised arm.

Her partner must place his hand in exactly the right place not just to support her correctly, but also to avoid causing her excruciating pain by catching her under the rib cage or squashing a kidney! Once again, an elegant and moving moment in classical ballet is far more difficult to execute than the audience will ever realize.

Swallow lift   This is one of the most difficult lifts and can be terrifying for the girl, because she naturally feels that if she tips forward, she will land on her head. More important than strength in the success of such a lift is the coordination between the partners. She must hold herself absolutely still and balanced in her *swallow*-like pose, while he turns slowly round. To do this he must have positioned his hands in just the right place on the hip bones. These are fairly visible on a slim dancer, and the teacher may explain to young students that this is exactly what they were designed for!

119

Pressage Lift   The *pressage* lift is one of the highest in ballet, and is frequently seen in contemporary as well as classical dance. In order to get so high off the ground, it is vital for the girl to help her partner by leaping off the ground with her lower leg just as he starts to lift her. Watching the *pressage* lift from the auditorium, one is probaby unaware that what looks to us like a straight forward lift for the boy, is actually a supported jump from the girl's point of view. Like all jumps it starts with a *plié* or *fondu* (second drawing).

This lift though similar to the previous one,

feels more secure because of the position of her partner's hands. If something goes wrong she can always put her foot down (in rehearsal at least). A common exercise for the partner to work on is to lift the girl straight up from an *arabesque,* without her doing a *plié* to help him. This would not be possible for a smallish man if his partner weighed more than eight stone.

To make the best of her little jump in performance, he bends his knees, straightens and locks his arms under her while she jumps. Then he can lift her the rest of the way by unbending his legs. It is, of course, far easier to

lift a heavy weight with the legs than with the arms, and weightlifters use the same technique once they have 'snatched' the weights up to shoulder level.

It is important to realize that dancers who try to increase their lifting ability by weight training alone are missing the point. Coordination and technique are far more important than brute strength, and the smaller male dancer can easily lift someone his own weight or more if he has that technique.

Fish Dive   The *fish dive* is one of the most spectacular displays in classical ballet. In the classroom example shown here, the girl is lowered into the *fish dive* from a supported *first arabesque* with her partner taking her weight on his thigh. In performance, this thigh is often hidden by her *tutu,* adding a feeling of danger to the effect.

Fish dives can follow a number of steps and lifts. In the *grand pas de deux* of THE SLEEPING BEAUTY we see Aurora fall twice into the *fish dive;* in the photograph above from a series of *pirouettes* and then, at the climax, she falls straight out of a high lift supported by one arm around her knees.

123

THE SLEEPING BEAUTY Aurora, who
never bowed to anyone before, sinks down in
homage to her prince. She is very vulnerable, as
he raises her up on to *pointe,* and supports her
while she brings her leg up through the *retiré,*
position into *attitude* (fig 3). He shows his
admiration and love by the noble and dramatic
way that he raises her, and then, when she is
perfectly balanced, steps back leaving her
proudly alone on *pointe* in a stunning *arabesque.*

Two of the great classical ballets that every
young dancer or ballet-goer is likely to see are
THE SLEEPING BEAUTY and SWAN LAKE. We have
already seen a number of examples from solos
and *pas de deux* from these two ballets. The
examples in the following fourteen pages have
been chosen to show the special quality of slow
supported *adage* movements.

124

THE SLEEPING BEAUTY This is a wedding *pas de deux,* the atmosphere is happy, and intimate. The choreography is noble and restrained at the beginning, building up to the more flamboyant high lifts and *fish dives* later on. As the Prince supports Princess Aurora with one hand, she *développés* her leg towards him and he raises his other arm to echo her *port de bras.* (first three drawings). She leans back as far as possible, then suddenly whips her body round finishing in a triumphant supported *attitude croiseé derrière* in a *fouetté.*

This fouetté requires even greater coordination between the dancers than any spectacular lift. It is a real feat of balance. Not only must she be well placed and perfectly on balance as she turns, but he must judge to perfection, the moment when he releases her hand, and transfers his support to her waist.

This *fouetté* is like a speeded-up version of the *fouetté of adage* on page 30.

SWAN LAKE: Mime Mime is a sign language which is often used in the older ballets where the complicated plot cannot be conveyed by dance alone. Simple naturalistic gestures, a hand over the heart for 'I love you', are easy to understand and have the same meaning in many different cultures. Other gestures which would have been understood by any theatre goer 100 years ago now need explaining to a modern audience.

I am   the **Queen** (crown)   of the **Swans**

Here is a well-known *mime* passage from SWAN LAKE, Act 2, which uses many of the more common gestures and is still retained in many modern productions. Princess Odette is telling Prince Siegfried that she and her companions have been put under an evil spell by the magician, Von Rothbart, who has changed them all into swans. Only if a man promises to marry Odette and love her forever will the spell be broken.

I can **see**

over there

129

*a lake of my mother's **tears***

one

if a man promises to ***love me***

and ***marry*** me

bad man turned me into a swan

but

and **swears** to love me forever

I shall be a Swan **no more**

SWAN LAKE In the White Swan *pas de deux*, Prince Siegfried is captivated by Odette, Queen of the Swans. She has already explained with the use of *mime* that she has been enchanted by an evil magician, and must remain half swan, half human, until she is released from his spell by someone promising to love and marry her. All her movements are sad, graceful and regal; he moves around her, trying to reassure her and demonstrate his love.

In the first four drawings, she slowly unfolds her leg (*développé*) and inclines with a swan-like gesture of the raised arm towards him, then yields, falling back almost as if he has deserted her. He steps towards her, catches her around the waist, and gently lowers her in the direction of her fall, while all the time protecting and supporting her.
(Continues)

133

134

Tchaikovsky's sad cello solo gives an air of tragic intensity to their movements, as Odette's wings surrender and brush, almost lifelessly, against the ground. But as Prince Siegfried raises her gently upwards, his love, and the knowledge that it will break the spell, seems to give her new hope. Her arms and leg rise gently into *arabesque,* and she relaxes for a moment into an *arabesque fondue*.

Different partnerships will bring their own interpretation to this special *pas de deux*.

Later in Swan Lake these same *adage* movements are mimicked and even at times, caricatured by Odile, the magician Von Rothbart's evil daughter. Both characters are, of course, danced by the same ballerina, giving her what is considered to be the greatest opportunity in classical ballet to demonstrate artistry and expressiveness.

SWAN LAKE   In the Black Swan *pas de deux* Odile flirts with Prince Siegfried who has fallen in love with her, believing her to be Odette. The wicked Odile tries to get him to betray Odette by asking her to marry him. Here in the Black Swan

pas de deux, she leaps teasingly away in a *grand jeté en tournant* ending in an *arabesque* which she follows by sinking, in mock submission, to the ground in a swan-like pose.

Finally class and rehearsal are ended, and the dancers have had at least two hours to rest. Now they are halfway through the evening, performance. The curtain is about to rise on the second act of SWAN LAKE. The murmur of the audience has died down, the house lights dim, and the orchestra begins to play. Dancers check each others' costumes and headdresses; fasten hooks and eyes, and adjust *pointe* shoes. The stage manager issues instructions to the stage hands through their headsets as they check the scenery. The working lights dim and smoke begins to pour onto the set. At the last moment the dancers hurry off stage to take up their positions in the wings, and the curtain rises on a deserted and misty lakeside scene.

Brief Glossary

Additional Terms often used in Classical Ballet and not otherwise explained in the text.

ADAGE (1) slow, flowing movements in solos or pas de deux
(2) section of class where these movements are practiced

ALLEGRO (1) lively, fast movements
(2) sections of class where these are practiced, subdivided into PETIT ALLEGRO (small jumps) and GRAND ALLEGRO (big turns and jumps)

AVANT, EN forwards

BEATS, BEATEN jumps where legs and feet cross over (see *entrechat*) or beat against each other (see *cabriole*)

CHOREOGRAPHY, CHOREOGRAPHER the art of composing new movements and steps, and linking them together, and the person who does so

CORPS DE BALLET any dancer in a ballet who is not one of the soloists

DERRIÈRE behind

ELEVATION (1) the ability to attain height in jumps
(2) a rare quality where a dancer gives a feeling of flight to jumps even when quite close to the ground

ENCHAÎNEMENT linking; a linking of two steps or more

EXTENSION the ability to raise and control a fully-extended leg in the air (see *grand jeté*)

GRAND PAS DE DEUX begins with an Adage for both dancers, continues with alternating solos for the girl and boy and ends with the Coda where they dance together again

PAS DE DEUX a dance for two people (*not* always a boy and girl)

PAS DE TROIS a dance for three people

PAS DE QUATRE a dance for four people

PORT DE BRAS (1) graceful movement of the arms through a series of positions
(2) Exercises in class designed to develop that quality

PREPARATION prepapatory movements for a step or jump; a pirouette may begin from a preparation in the fourth position.

RELEVÉ lifted or raised up. Rising up onto pointe on one or both feet, either as a smooth continuous movement or with a little spring. Most familiar in Second, Fourth and Fifth positions, in attitude and in arabesque.

RETIRÉ drawing the toe up to the level of the other knee

SUPPORTING LEG } A dancer stands on the
WORKING LEG } *supporting leg,* while moving the *working leg*

Index

Photograph credits